Now It Is
WINTER

For Eileen and Lee
and Elvira and Joe
—E. S.

For Connor, Sean, and Katherine
—M. N. D.

Written by ©2004 Eileen Spinelli
Illustrated by ©2004 Mary Newell DePalma

Published 2004 by Eerdmans Books for Young Readers
An imprint of Wm. B. Eerdmans Publishing Company
255 Jefferson S.E., Grand Rapids, Michigan 49503
P.O. Box 163, Cambridge CB3 9PU U.K.

Printed and bound in China
05 06 07 08 09 10 7 6 5 4 3 2
ISBN 0-8028-5244-0
A catalog record of this book is available from the Library of Congress.

The illustrations were rendered in acrylic and cut paper.
The display type was set in Kepler and Georgia.
The text type was set in Georgia.
Art Director Gayle Brown
Graphic Design Matthew Van Zomeren

Now It Is
WINTER

Written by Eileen Spinelli
Illustrated by Mary Newell DePalma

Eerdmans Books for Young Readers
Grand Rapids, Michigan • Cambridge, U.K.

Will spring ever come?
Will the morning sun splash me awake?
Will it puddle the ducks on my pillow
with light?
Ever again?

Yes, spring will come.
But now it is winter.
Now there is the fuzzy dark
at the window.
And the morning moon grown pale.
And a few stray stars.
Say hello!

Will spring ever come?
Will there be black raspberries and cream
in my breakfast bowl?
Blackberries I helped pick?
Ever again?

Yes, there will be
blackberries and spring.
But now it is winter.
Now there is oatmeal
in your breakfast bowl.
With butter and brown sugar.
So delicious.
Taste it!

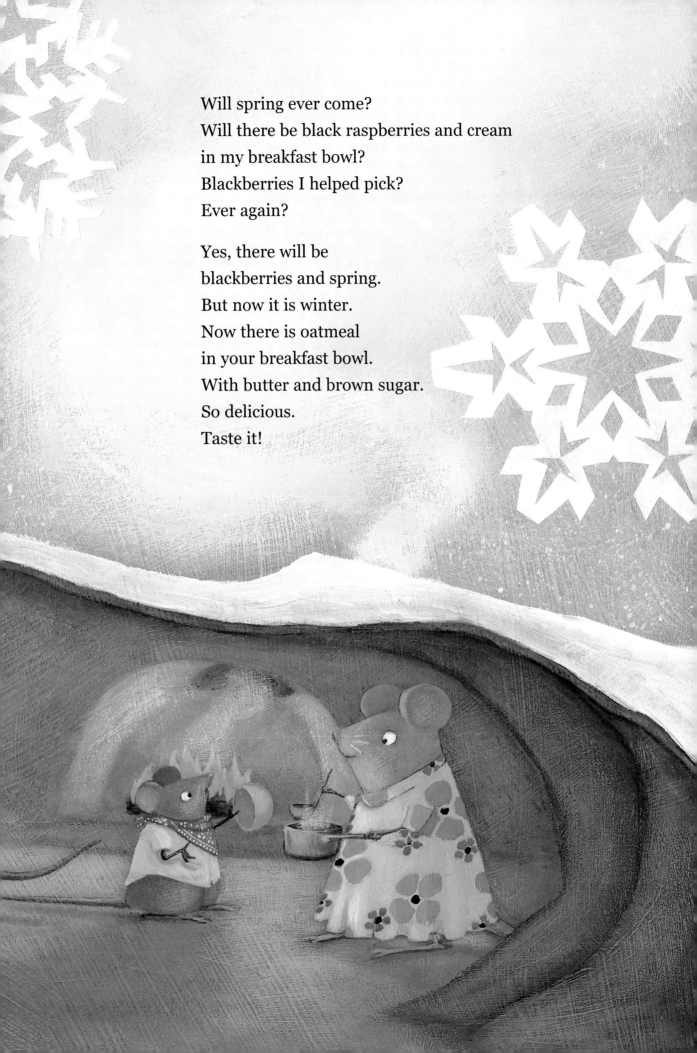

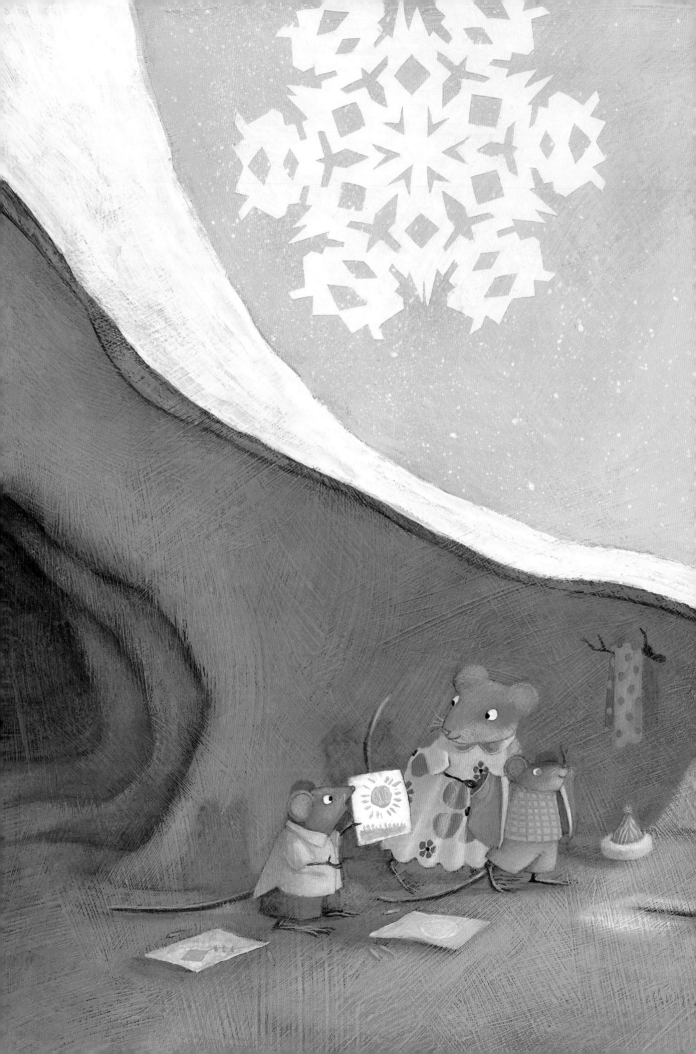

Will spring ever come?
Will I roll down steep grassy hills
giggling towards the bottom?
Ever again?

Yes, spring will come
and grass and giggles too.

But now it is winter.
Now you can sail downhill
on your sled
lifted on snowy laughter.
What fun!

Will spring ever come?
Will I help Grandma gather
dandelions and daisies?
Will we look for garden fairies
near the stone wall?
Ever again?

Yes, spring will come
to you and Grandma and the fairies.

But now it is winter.
Now pinecones are for gathering.
Here is a basket.
Now snow angels nap near the stone wall.
Shhhh!
Tiptoe past.

Will spring ever come?
Will the robin return
to nest in the tree
Dad planted
when I was born?
Ever again?

Yes, spring will bring the robin back.
But now it is winter.
Now the bright cardinal
flashes red against the sky,
swoops to a leafless branch.
How pretty!
Come see.

Will spring ever come?
Will I play tag with my friends
in the park
racing and chasing?
Ever again?

Yes, you will race and chase come spring.
But now it is winter.

Now you can carry your skates
to the frozen pond.
Your friends are ice-dancing there
to the music of the wind.
Swirling . . . twirling.
You twirl too!

Will spring ever come?
Will you and I make paper kites?
Fly them down an April band of beach?
Ever again?

Yes, spring will come and beach and kites.
But now it is winter.
Now you and I shall make a snowman.
Here is a carrot for his nose.
Two buttons for eyes.
Isn't he handsome?
What shall we name him?

Will spring ever come?
Will I hear the sleepy sound
of soft rain
pattering on the roof?
Ever again?

Yes, there will be spring and rain.
But now it is winter.
Now sleet twinkles down
sprinkling the roof.
It sounds like silver.
Listen!

Will spring ever come?
Will the night sky grow pink
and the night breeze whisper . . .

Hush, child. Hush.

Spring will come all pink sky and breezes.
But now . . . now it is winter.
Now you are cozy in your flannel pajamas.
And warm in your bed.

Now is good—
as in "goodnight"—
and sweet—
as in "sweet dreams."

Now is the blessing.
Now is the time to love.
Now is the time
to be.